Questions and Answers About
THE GOLD RUSH

BRIANNA BATTISTA

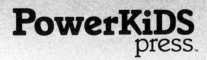

PowerKiDS press.

NEW YORK

Published in 2019 by The Rosen Publishing Group, Inc.
29 East 21st Street, New York, NY 10010

First Edition

Editor: Brianna Battista
Book Design: Michael Flynn

Photo Credits: Cover American School/Getty Images; cover, pp. 1, 3–24, 26–28, 30–32 (background texture) NuConcept Dezine/Shutterstock.com; p. 5 © Ivy Close Images/Alamy; p. 6 Library of Congress/Corbis Historical/Getty Images; pp. 7, 9, 11, 13, 21 courtesy of California State Library; pp. 8, 20 courtesy of the Library of Congress; p. 12 https://en.wikipedia.org/wiki/James_K._Polk#/media/File:James_Knox_Polk_by_GPA_Healy,_1858.jpg; p. 15 courtesy of Oakland Museum of California; p. 17 https://commons.wikimedia.org/wiki/File:California_Clipper_500.jpg; p. 19 Fotosearch/Archive Photos/Getty Images; p. 23 Time Life Pictures/The Life Picture Collection/Getty Images; p. 25 © North Wind Picture Archive; p. 26 Everett Historical/Shutterstock.com; p. 27 Huntington Library/SuperStock; p. 29 Hulton Archive/Archive Photos/Getty Images, p. 30 MarcelClemens/Shutterstock.com.

Library of Congress Cataloging-in-Publication Data

Names: Battista, Brianna.
Title: Questions and answers about the Gold Rush / Brianna Battista.
Description: New York : PowerKids Press, 2019. | Series: Eye on historical
   sources | Includes index.
Identifiers: LCCN 2018006971| ISBN 9781538341193 (library bound) | ISBN
   9781538341209 (pbk.) | ISBN 9781538341216 (6 pack)
Subjects: LCSH: California–Gold discoveries–Juvenile literature. | Gold
   mines and mining–California–History–19th century–Juvenile literature.
Classification: LCC F865 .B325 2019 | DDC 979.4/04–dc23
LC record available at https://lccn.loc.gov/2018006971

Manufactured in the United States of America

CPSIA Compliance Information: Batch #CS18PK: For Further Information contact Rosen Publishing, New York, New York at 1-800-237-9932

CONTENTS

DREAMS OF TREASURE

When you think about gold, what comes to mind? You might think of a wedding ring, a gold medal, or maybe even buried treasure. One thing is certain—gold is precious and always in **demand**.

In an 1848 issue of the *New York Herald*, Americans read there was a gold rush going on way out west at a place called Sutter's Mill in California. After hearing this news, hundreds of thousands of people from all over the world decided to try their luck and make the trip. Between 1848 and the mid-1850s, California's population nearly tripled to almost half a million people. But did most people get what they came for? Did they find gold and strike it rich?

IN THE 1800s, TRAVEL WAS DONE ON FOOT, BY HORSE, OR BY BOAT. THE JOURNEY OUT WEST WAS A RISKY AND DANGEROUS ONE.

THE GOLDEN GORGE

The rush for gold began in Coloma, California. On January 24, 1848, a handyman named James Wilson Marshall was going about his business. He was working for his employer, John Sutter, and looking over the construction of a sawmill. What Marshall found in the river near the mill that day would change both men's lives—and that of the entire country—forever. Marshall had found gold.

Sources from the Past

Primary sources are original documents created during the time period being studied. Historians believe Marshall drew the picture on page 7 shortly after he discovered gold. This makes it a primary source for the gold rush. Primary sources help us understand history and lead to better study skills. What else can we learn from Marshall's drawing?

JAMES WILSON MARSHALL

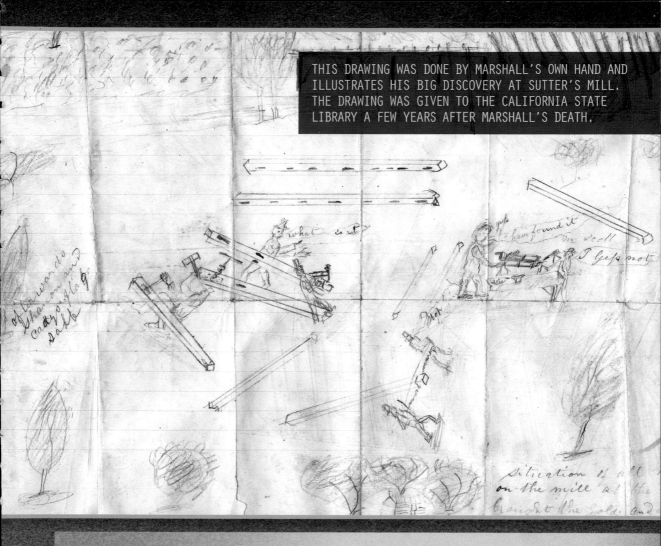

THIS DRAWING WAS DONE BY MARSHALL'S OWN HAND AND ILLUSTRATES HIS BIG DISCOVERY AT SUTTER'S MILL. THE DRAWING WAS GIVEN TO THE CALIFORNIA STATE LIBRARY A FEW YEARS AFTER MARSHALL'S DEATH.

After the discovery, Marshall quickly went to find Sutter and tell him the news. Sutter didn't believe it at first but quickly changed his mind when Marshall put the gold on a nearby table. The two men went down to the sawmill, and Sutter examined the site himself, using his knife to cut out yet another lump of gold from a nearby **gorge**.

GOLD VS. LUMBER

John Sutter was a Swiss businessman who came to America to make his fortune. He planned to build a town but was building a sawmill first so people would have lumber. Sutter had trouble finding enough people to work on the land, a problem that would soon be solved as thousands of people began **emigrating** west in the 1840s.

JOHN SUTTER

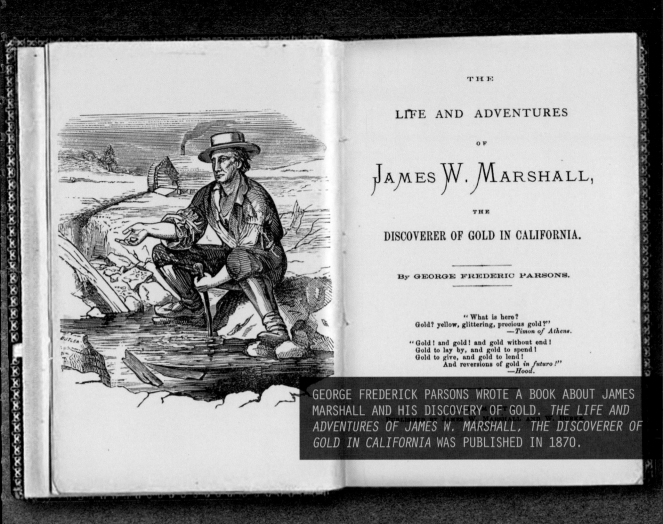

THE

LIFE AND ADVENTURES

OF

JAMES W. MARSHALL,

THE

DISCOVERER OF GOLD IN CALIFORNIA.

By GEORGE FREDERIC PARSONS.

"What is here?
Gold? yellow, glittering, precious gold?"
—*Timon of Athens.*

"Gold! and gold! and gold without end!
Gold to lay by, and gold to spend!
Gold to give, and gold to lend!
And reversions of gold *in futuro!*"
—*Hood.*

GEORGE FREDERICK PARSONS WROTE A BOOK ABOUT JAMES MARSHALL AND HIS DISCOVERY OF GOLD. *THE LIFE AND ADVENTURES OF JAMES W. MARSHALL, THE DISCOVERER OF GOLD IN CALIFORNIA* WAS PUBLISHED IN 1870.

Marshall and Sutter had hoped to keep the discovery of gold secret. Sutter was in the process of gaining a longer **lease** of the land and didn't want to slow down the construction of the mill. However, keeping the gold a secret proved impossible. Some Native American workers had also found gold, and the news soon spread throughout the land.

GOLD FEVER

In 1848, word of Marshall's discovery started finding its way throughout California. At the mill itself, men working for Sutter left their jobs to search for gold along the American River. In May of that year, news of the discovery of gold reached San Francisco. There was even a **sample** of gold dust displayed in public.

"Gold fever" hit hard, and large numbers of prospectors, or miners, began traveling to the area. News of the gold spread slowly throughout the United States, across the Atlantic Ocean to Europe, south into Mexico and South America, and west across the Pacific Ocean by way of trading ships. The news of Marshall's discovery would lead to a huge population increase.

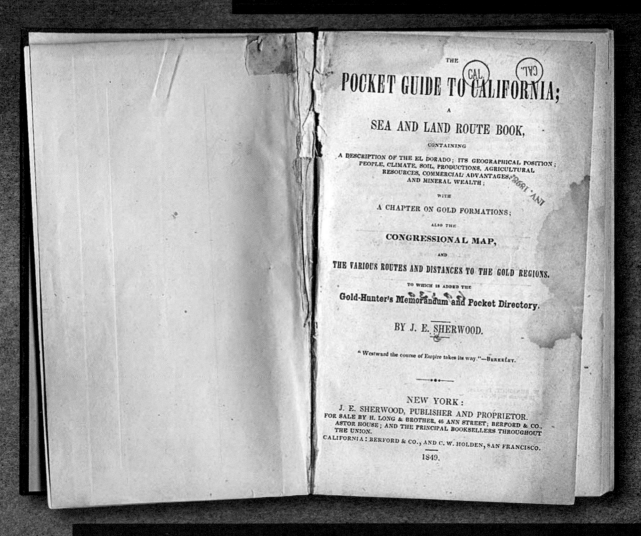

THE

POCKET GUIDE TO CALIFORNIA;

A

SEA AND LAND ROUTE BOOK,

CONTAINING

A DESCRIPTION OF THE EL DORADO; ITS GEOGRAPHICAL POSITION;
PEOPLE, CLIMATE, SOIL, PRODUCTIONS, AGRICULTURAL
RESOURCES, COMMERCIAL ADVANTAGES,
AND MINERAL WEALTH;

WITH

A CHAPTER ON GOLD FORMATIONS;

ALSO THE

CONGRESSIONAL MAP,

AND

THE VARIOUS ROUTES AND DISTANCES TO THE GOLD REGIONS.

TO WHICH IS ADDED THE

Gold-Hunter's Memorandum and Pocket Directory.

BY J. E. SHERWOOD.

"Westward the course of Empire takes its way."—BERKELEY.

NEW YORK:
J. E. SHERWOOD, PUBLISHER AND PROPRIETOR.
FOR SALE BY H. LONG & BROTHER, 46 ANN STREET; BERFORD & CO.,
ASTOR HOUSE; AND THE PRINCIPAL BOOKSELLERS THROUGHOUT
THE UNION.
CALIFORNIA: BERFORD & CO., AND C. W. HOLDEN, SAN FRANCISCO.

1849.

Sources from the Past

This book by J. Ely Sherwood is a primary source because it was written during the gold rush, within months of Marshall's discovery. Its full title is *The Pocket Guide to California; A Sea and Land Route Book, Containing a Description of the El Dorado . . . To Which Is Added the Gold-Hunter's Memorandum and Pocket Directory.*

COULD IT REALLY BE TRUE?

When people in the eastern United States first heard word of gold in California, they didn't believe the stories. The *New York Herald* reported news of the gold strike in August, but President James K. Polk didn't officially announce it was true until December 5, 1848.

Within days of Polk's announcement, the people of the eastern United States became swept up in gold fever. It was all that many people could think about, talk about, and write about. For some, the only cure for the fever was to head west to seek their fortune. Men who made the journey later returned to the East Coast to give speeches on the subject, which stirred up even more interest in California.

JAMES K. POLK

CARRIERS' ADDRESS

TO THE PATRONS OF

THE EASTERN ARGUS.

JANUARY 1, 1849.

Sources from the Past

Primary sources can tell us how people felt about events when they were occurring. For example, many saw gold fever as an illness affecting the morality of the entire nation. In "Carriers' Address," the writer shares the idea that gold seekers were forgetting about the important things in life. It was true that many men who headed west to seek gold often left their families behind. Sometimes they left good jobs behind, too, hoping it would all be worth it in the end.

EXTRA, EXTRA!

Only a few months had passed since James Marshall discovered gold, but hopeful gold seekers had all types of written sources about it at their fingertips. Books were published within months. Newspapers around the country jumped at the chance to use gold fever to sell papers in the winter of 1848 to 1849. The newspapers published story after story about the adventures of life out west, using every detail they could to fill their pages.

There were many personal accounts of ship **passengers** and captains who made the trip to California. There were stories from the goldfields by those already hard at work digging for riches. There were also tales of wealth beyond one's wildest dreams. All this stirred up even more energy for people who wanted to get to California.

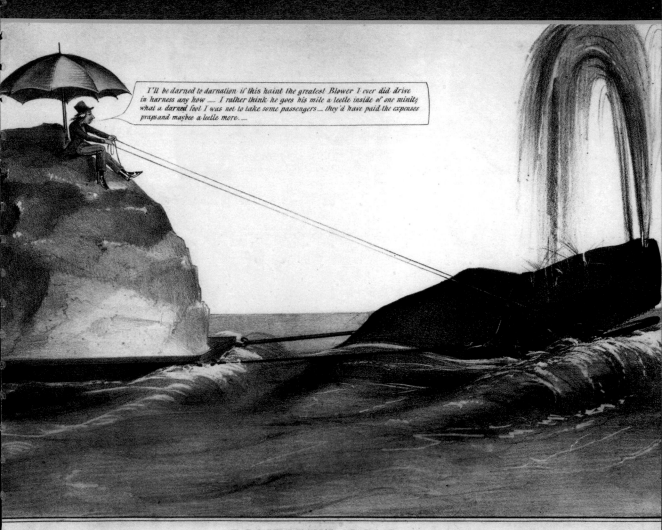

THE NEWSPAPERS WERE ALSO FULL OF IMAGES AND COMMENTS POKING FUN AT THE **OBSESSION** WITH CALIFORNIA'S GOLD. THIS PIECE BY NATHAN CURRIER CALLED "CALIFORNIA GOLD" WAS PRINTED IN 1849.

AND THEY'RE OFF!

Once gold fever hit the East Coast, there was no stopping it. Easterners headed out west were often called forty-niners because of the year, 1849. Some took ships and sailed south, down the coast, around the southern tip of South America, and then up the Pacific coast to reach San Francisco Bay. An estimated 16,000 people traveled to California using this route in 1849, followed by about 12,000 more people in 1850.

The trip to California by sea was **difficult**, and not just because of the ocean. Many passengers got very sick on board. One common illness was scurvy, which was caused by a lack of vitamin C. It was difficult to keep a supply of vitamin C–rich fruits and vegetables on ships because these foods quickly went bad.

Sources from the Past

This advertisement for tickets aboard a ship sailing to San Francisco is a primary source. Notice the use of the word "**elegant**" several times. The ad may have tried to appeal to upper-class people. The price for a ticket was very high for the times, even though passengers lived in very small rooms on these ships. What else can we learn by looking at this ad?

THE OREGON TRAIL

Gold was not the only thing that brought Americans to California. Years before Marshall ever found his gold, people from the East Coast had been making their way west. They mapped out routes across the continent toward California as well as Oregon. These pioneers came to be known as overlanders, and the route they most often took was called the Oregon Trail.

After gold was found, the trail started to become crowded with forty-niners that didn't want to take a ship—or could not afford a ticket—to California. It was a very difficult journey. Just like on the ocean, sickness took many lives and bad weather often took many more. Living conditions on the Oregon Trail were very poor.

THIS IMAGE BY HENRY R. ROBINSON MAKES FUN OF TRAVELERS WHO TOOK THE DIFFICULT ROUTE ACROSS THE COUNTRY TO GET TO CALIFORNIA. MANY OF THEM HAD VERY LITTLE EXPERIENCE. ▶

Sources from the Past

Robinson's image from about 1850 shows a man on his way out west, loaded down with lots of items. Forty-niners with no experience would often pack way more than they needed. They usually had to dump things along the trail to lighten their loads. What are some of the items the man is the man is carrying? Do you think they'd be helpful on the long journey to California?

A GOLD HUNTER ON HIS WAY TO CALIFORNIA, VIA, St. LOUIS.

Published by H.R.Robinson 31 Park Row N.York

THE BAY IS BOOMING

In the months and years after Marshall discovered gold at Sutter's Mill, San Francisco became the go-to place for prospectors all over the world. Before Marshall's discovery, San Francisco had been a quiet little port with a population of around 1,000 people. Just a few years later, it had grown into a booming city of nearly 30,000 people—most of whom were gold seekers.

SUTTER'S MILL

San Francisco didn't go through the many years of growth and progress that most cities usually experience. Instead, it became an instant city of tents and wooden structures. The prospectors who arrived at San Francisco Bay often wanted to start looking for gold right away, so these structures were built quickly and only provided the most basic shelter.

LIFE AS A MINER

The average miner didn't have an easy life. The first mining camps sprang up immediately after Marshall's discovery at Sutter's Mill. These groups of tents were set up around the miners' claims. A claim was an area of land that had been taken over by a miner as his own. Rising with the sun, miners would eat a small breakfast of biscuits and coffee, and then spend the day digging for gold with picks and shovels. They worked long hours and often found very little gold.

When the sun set, the miners would return to their tents for dinner, which was usually pickled meat and coffee. When the sun went down, there was little to do but go to bed or play card games and drink by the fire.

THE MINERS SHOWN HERE ARE CRADLING FOR GOLD. CRADLING IS A SLOW PROCESS IN WHICH GOLD IS SEPARATED FROM DIRT. THERE WAS A FASTER PROCESS CALLED PANNING, BUT MINERS OFTEN FOUND A LITTLE MORE GOLD EACH DAY WHEN CRADLING.

THE WILD, WILD WEST

The promise of better lives brought thousands to California, but the **reality** of bad behavior became a problem for many of the miners. Some set aside their principles and acted in ways they would've never dreamed of before. Good men were suddenly letting greed, and not higher principles, take the lead in their actions.

Bandits traveled around the region stealing what they liked from those who either couldn't protect themselves or found themselves up against too many at once. There were no police officers to make sure the laws were followed and no real jails to hold offenders. There was always the possibility of danger in and around the mining camps. If a miner found gold, he might also find himself in trouble.

THIS HAND-COLORED WOODCUT SHOWS SAN FRANCISCO IN THE 1850s WHEN BANDITS WERE A BIG PROBLEM FOR THE MINERS.

25

STRETCHED TRUTHS

The miners soon learned the tales of finding large pieces of gold were likely just stories. Days, weeks, or months might pass before a miner found any gold at all. In the meantime, the miner would have to find another way to make a living. Men from the East Coast who had left their well-paying jobs now found themselves doing whatever jobs they could find in exchange for food and lodging.

SAN FRANCISCO, 1851

The life of riches the emigrants had imagined rarely matched their real lives. Those prospectors who did manage to gain some wealth would often send the money back home to their families. Companies began to spring up that allowed the forty-niners to **transfer** money safely from California to points throughout the country. Modern banking was beginning to take shape.

EXPERIENCING NEW CULTURES

California had become home to large numbers of Chinese, Mexican, Australian, and Latin American **immigrants**. These are just a few of the many groups of people that came to California in search of gold and a better life. Americans from the East Coast who had gone west for gold often blamed California's problems on immigrants whose **culture** they didn't understand. Many immigrants were wrongly accused of crimes and then killed simply because their skin wasn't white.

In the early 1850s, laws were passed requiring immigrant miners to pay for a mining permit each month. Laws like this, along with the dangers they faced each day, were enough to make many immigrants return to their home countries. Those who stayed often left the mining cities and found work on farms instead.

DIFFERENT CULTURES HAD A TOUGH TIME UNDERSTANDING EACH OTHER. THIS PHOTOGRAPH SHOWS A CHINESE PROSPECTOR WORKING ALONGSIDE AN AMERICAN PROSPECTOR.

29

LASTING EFFECTS

The possibility of striking it rich that had brought hopeful miners from all over the world to California soon began to lose its luster. Some people's dreams had been realized, and they'd come out with their golden prize. But most people's dreams faded away, replaced with the realities of rough living and few results.

Within just a few years of James Marshall's discovery of gold at Sutter's Mill, fewer and fewer people came to California. By the mid-1850s, many mining camps looked like ghost towns. Although the gold rush had happened just a few years before, people now told stories about what life had been like back then, when the possibility of finding gold was all that mattered. For many, it had quickly become a distant memory.

GLOSSARY

culture: The beliefs and ways of life of a group of people.

demand: A strong request for something.

difficult: Not easy.

elegant: Graceful and attractive.

emigrate: To leave a country or region to live somewhere else.

gorge: A deep, narrow area between hills or mountains.

immigrant: A person who comes to a country to live there.

lease: A lawful agreement that lets someone use something, such as land, for a period of time in return for payment.

obsession: A state in which someone is always thinking about someone or something.

passenger: A person who is traveling from one place to another in a car, train, ship, bus, or airplane, and who is not driving or working on it.

reality: The true situation that exists.

sample: A small amount of something that gives people information about the thing it was taken from.

transfer: To move something or someone from one place to another.

INDEX

WEBSITES

Due to the changing nature of Internet links, PowerKids Press has developed an online list of websites related to the subject of this book. This site is updated regularly. Please use this link to access the list: www.powerkidslinks.com/eohs/gold